THE COWS
WHO PLAYED

BINGO!

THE COWS who PLAYED BINGO

DORSET in POETRY, ART and TALE

by

Sue Worth

First published by Sue Worth in association with Firkin Publishing, Dorset
November 2017

Printed and bound in the UK by
Remous Print, Sherborne, Dorset

ISBN 978-0-9551633-4-0

Contents

About the author. vi
Acknowledgements vi

PART 1

My Place. 2
An Abused Wife's Prayer 3
Young Mother. 4
Great Grandmother 6
Tick Tock 7
Poacher 8
Granny Collins' House 9
Weymouth Maid. 10
Empty Vessels 11
The Cut of Me Jib 12

PART 2

Dorset Ophelier 14
I before E 16
The West Country Ages of Man 17
Mornin, Maister 18
Incomer. 19
Reuben 20
Arringe Juice an Moosli. 22
Ethelred the Unready 24
Melchior 26

PART 3

The Cows Who Played Bingo 28
The Colorado Beetle Craze 31
The Good Shepherd 34
The Drowners in the Water Meadow. 36
Hiring Fair: Isaac Hallet, shepherd, and his collie 38
Party Pieces. 39

About the author

Sue Worth is a Performance Poet and Storyteller who has acted and written for The New Hardy Players. Her poetry has been published in *The Countryman*, an Arts Council Anthology, and broadcast on BBC Radio 4 and Solent Radio.

Born in 1951 into a Dorset awash with stories, weary of austerity and soundly rooted in its own history, Sue spent her childhood in the village of Stratton – and feels it well spent, as she has always loved stories. Sue has worked in West Dorset hospitals as Carer, on Clinical Audits within Intensive Care, and as Manager of a clinical system in an I.T. Department.

Sue is married to Andy, who has always supported her writing. They have three children, and their daughter Naomi is an artist, who, with Liz Poulain, has contributed the stunning illustrations for this book.

Acknowledgements

Very many thanks to Liz Bennett for her encouragement, persistence and skill in putting this beautiful book together for me.

To Liz and my fabulous daughter Naomi Price for their stunning artwork that so captures the spirit of my stories.

To Tim Laycock, Kate Clanchy, Jane McKell, Paul Hyland, and others who have critiqued and encouraged my writing.

To Brian and Joy Caddy, Andy Venton, and Ian Condon for lending their voices as a model for characters, and performing with me as I polished these poems and stories.

To my husband Andy for his support of my writing and for producing a CD of 'The Cows Who Played Bingo', with recordings of real Dorset Voices. I would like to thank Brian Caddy for his matchless performances of 'Arringe Juice n' Moosli' and other pieces, which he has performed, along with his own work, across Dorset.

To Naomi, Greg and Matthew for so often being the first sounding board for my stories. To Lil Puckett, whose tales of Dorset fostered my love of storytelling, and to all those who shared their stories or listened to mine. Thank you.

Part 1

The Dorset voices telling their stories in the following pages slide, as I slide myself, from 'talking proper' to accent to dialect and back again. We've aimed to capture the rhythms and richness of our Dorset English in a book that is beautiful, uncluttered and a joy to read, so, for example, apostrophes to replace the beginning or end of words have been used sparingly.

While Dorset can be a gabble, it is more often drawn out and unhurried, apt to wander, and used to taking its own good time.

My Place

My place lies unrecognised
Under the clutter of others lives.
Loving still their loud clamour and newly
discarded enthusiasms. Elusive, under layers

my place lies. Exquisite
ordered, quiet and enclosed.
A garden, water running over warmed
stone into deep green pools, stirred
by pairs of sinuous enamelled fish.

A sunlit, open sprawl of rooms.
With books and beautiful unbroken things
displayed and delicate as day. My place.
Time stands untyranted serving only me.

Won Solent Radio competition, judged by Kate Clanchy

An Abused Wife's Prayer

I don't ask that his brakes should fail, Lord.

Only, if this is the day someone's brakes
must fail while they're riding down Boot Hill
at full speed and they're killed amongst the traffic
at the bottom, when nobody helps.

Let it be him.

Young Mother

In the country,
People are ashamed of poverty.
Hate the neighbours to see them managing badly.

The day-to-day counting of pennies on an agricultural wage,
stretching food, saving fuel, wearing jumble-sale clothes with
shoes that leak, second-rate education, sub-standard housing and
a bus that runs twice a week.

That's not poverty, nor even being poor.
They riot in the city so they get a little more.
Who riots in the country? We can safely be ignored.

I'm not even supposed to say.
Poverty for her has to be absolute –
No food, no clothes, no fire.
No roof above your head.

Dead from starvation, that's her definition a poverty.

I only asked for help once –
The time he was out of work and wouldn't claim.
You hear such stories of people on the social
and I only wanted coats for the kids.

You don't know the effort it took me
to walk through that door.

I explained … we must have saved them
hundreds of pounds and more.

She said, "You can't afford pride in your position."
God, she was lucky to be inside that little glass box.

"Tell that to 'is family," I cried
"I'm expected to feed and clothe them
on pride an' pretty scenery."

An' then I went back. An' I managed again.

Great Grandmother

Oah yes, life's much easier now.
I'd ate to ave to go back t' them days.
People ave got more now than we ever dreamt possible.
Mind you, zometimes the more they ave,
the more they want an' the less they're 'appy with.

Take er that's married to my Grandzon.
I'd 'ave give my eye teeth for alf
what she's got when mine were zmall.
She gives them such ideas.
They got to learn – you can't ave it all.

Poverty! An 'er wi' a fridge,
an' a washin machine, an' a telly.
She watches too much telly, if you ask me,
that's 'alf the trouble.

I do love the children –
to see them so well fed an 'ealthy.
I don't begrudge them, except
it does make me angry when they do say,
"Nan, I'm freezin, I'm starvin ungry."

Freezin is five to a bed wi
a cwoat thrown over you come winter,
an starvation's not the same as greed.

I feel for the poor chap.
All is ard work ... an she shames im
wi all this talk of poverty.

I know they'll never be rich
but they manage nicely.

Tick Tock

You never eard im referred to as old Tick Tock before?
I am surprised – I thought you knew everything about this village.
– Fear makes a man sly, his humour underhand
but they ad too much to lose to risk offending –
you have to understand.
So – it's a habit of the working man to give nicknames, both to a Master
and each other, so they may talk with a little more honesty
during the working day.
So – this is how old Tick Tock got is name.

He was in the habit of timing the men,
with a great, gold pocket watch.
He would stand there surveying them – weighing time in his hand.

One day, he brought his youngest son –
His favourite, fathered late in life.

The child grew restless with the cold –
Took hold the father's sleeve.
Would you believe – him – stooping – speaking gently,

"Only a little longer –
See my watch, now put it to your ear – can you hear the Tick Tock."

The men could hardly contain themselves –
Tick Tock!
An old tyrant – and baby talk.

Poacher

True I have a certain talent.
Though it's not for a man to
puff himself up like a cock bantum
as some soft creature up at the big 'ouse might.

The kingdom of Heaven shall come
like a thief in the night. Many's the
time I think upon this, as I crouch
in the wooded half-light.

Should the magistrates call me ignorant,
then I would say – I have read my Bible
closer than they. I know where my duty lies –
Why else has God given me this talent? I
take only what we need. I kill swiftly and
never make game of a fellow creature's suffering.

I ought to know how landowners judge me
when I am caught. Yet, how can a man be
said to steal that which is truly his? I take only
of my inheritance, seeded to me through Adam –
and here is irony – for they have been stealing from me
for centuries, yet cannot think the common man remembers.

I am not such a fool as to look for justice
from 'Society'. It always was one rule for them,
another for us. Just as in the time of the Tolpuddle Men –
sent to Australia for taking an oath, while the squires
and the one-legged paddlers were making hay,
and swearing their corrupted souls away.

If you still need more evidence – consider this:
When the rabbit was a great pest – and did untold
damage to crops, hungry people were still not allowed
to take them for food. Landowners begrudged
the very vermin to their own countrymen – While in town
and ostentatious as the Pharisee – they gave to good works
and Charity.

One legged paddlers – Freemasons

Granny Collins' House

In Granny Collins' House
They lead you up the stairs.
Past whitewashed walls
Into the room where it is always winter.

Then they whisper in the corner –
Such conversation being thought
Unfit for children.

Men are not allowed here.
We are to be burned by fear
So we never touch the fire again.

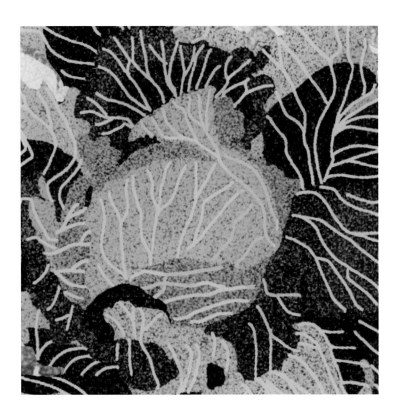

Weymouth Maid

My youngest son an thik Weymouth maid,
they'm ill-matched as chalk an cheese,
wi er thik single-minded she do zactly
As she please, an do mock the comely virtues
Of a simple country wife. But when I counselled
caution – Why, what do Feyther know a life?

I verbad un to go courtin,
they still courted on the sly,
the serpent whisperin to defy the Feyther.

Then,
when I heard of their deceitfulness,
I raged out into my garden, an thik
girt wold fool, Bill Samways, ups an says
"You'd as well verbid a vire to burn,
or birds to roost in trees as verbid
young love to vlourish in its season."

I verbad un to be married.
But they married just the same.
They flew out into their futures
singin out each other's name.

Forever yoked together
yet convinced that they was free
– as free as skylarks mating in mid winter.

An now – why now, they're livin wi I
fer they ad no place to bide
– an Lord knows,
love has all too short a season.

Thik – that
Bide – stay/dwell

Empty Vessels

Empty vessels, little Maidy,
Empty vessels.

They'm gossips –
don't you pay em any mind.
They'd ruin any reputation –
My son won't listen to women
,of that kind.

We saw you join the tiddy arvest
An boot-raw drag you weary ome.
We saw you stubborn, wi your poor hands
an back unused to vield work
As you refused to ever miss one day.

We watched you when you worked against the rain
Turnin time an time again to help some other woman.

That's why you ave bin give that extra sack of spuds
An we won't hear any different!

Come winter
when we'm sittin round the fire
eatin they baked tiddies for our tea

I shall say,
Now, we must thank our little Maidy
for this good food an for takin care of we.

Empty Vessels – an they'll sound against some other soul
later on today.

The Cut of Me Jib

The Jib of my imagining is sagging.
And it's frayed.
And, however manufactured, it's been
years since it was made.
And the cut that my Jib cuts –
Well, it needs cutting once again.

The general location of the Jib still puzzles me.
But I thought, as Jibs are judged,
it must be possible to see.
So I looked full in the mirror, and I tacked from side to side,
examined me both fore and aft, to
find where me Jib mid be. But, no matter, mind,
how hard I tried, two facts remained the same –
one, the elusive nature of the Jib,
and two, the cruel effects of gravity upon the human frame.

So. The Jib of my imagining is sagging and it's frayed.
But if I had my Jib trimmed and cut – Well, t'would only fray again.

And perhaps I like to think it frayed, and feel it matches me –
less at mercy from the elements than when first I went to sea.

Part 2

Dorset Ophelier

Ophelier. 'Phelier.
Do you get down off thik branch, maid,
swayin about over a swolled up river like that there.
Taint never safe.

Poor lamb,
Er's not got the sense she was born wi.

Ophelier,
If you baint careful,
You'm gonna to fall in an drown
'Fore you've a chance to kill thyself proper.

MERCY · 01 · OPHELIA WEPT

I before E

My father was a droll, quick-witted sort
of chap, famous for it in our village.
One day I was practising some
spellings, I'd got in an awful tangle,
and so sought his advice. "Dad," I called out.
"Is it I before E except after C, or E before I,
What's best? E before I or I before E."

He paused for the shortest time, then
answered, "Well, that depends.
I'd say I before Ee if it's time for tea
but Ee before I if it's my turn to buy."
I thought it was the cleverest thing
I'd ever heard. I repeated it all evening
and couldn't wait to try it out at school.

What a disappointment!
The teacher made I write out fifty times
*My father's advice to me on this occasion
was both morally suspect and grammatically unsound.*
Put I off spelling fer life.

The West Country Ages of Man

I met with a friend, and we
found ourselves over coffee talking
about the tragedy of her fast-approaching fifty
and the peculiarities of feeling it unleashed. She
said she was increasingly drawn to consider the
Shakespearean seven ages of man. And it came
to me of a sudden, and I replied, that in the
West Country, there are only *three* ages of man,
Baby, Old Enough To Know Better and
– Silly Old Sod!

Mornin, Maister

Oah, he's only pleadin poverty.
I tell thee it's a bad year
When ee don't ave a new car.

Mornin, Maister – nother fine day.
Ah, backsides to you, Maister – may
you fall an break yer neck!

Ee hates it when I call un 'Maister'
That's why I da do it.
An fer honesty's sake.
Ee is my Maister atter all
as surely as if ee owned I.

What you silly lot getting so excited
bout a good arvest for? Precious
little you'll see of it. I tell thee, I ope
every one a they blasteed tiddies do get blighted –
then I shan't ave to pick the buggers up come Autumn.

Ang on, ee's comin back
– best look like we're doin zummat.

Zummat – something

Incomer

Incomer they call me –
Incomer, Outsider, Townie,
Look What The Tide's Brought In.

Addlehead, Emmett –
Each year, the swarms of them
Plagued by the swarms of them.

Foreigner, Grockle,
The Cuckoo Maid, Leach, Mixen Low,
Oh – and they pause to say,
"We're pitifully short of teachers this way."

Emmet – ant
Grockle – insulting name for holiday makers/incomers
Mixen – dung heap

Reuben

The obscenities will have to go, Reuben,
You'll have to mend your ways –
The gambling, spitting – lewd suggestions.
Respectable women come into pubs these days.

…and the clothes – they're marvellous, of course.
Very traditional, a bit of history – but well,
you must realise how much they smell.

Just clean up a bit and the tourists will love you.
What a character! With all those wonderful stories
– the suitable ones anyway. They'll probably
buy you a drink or two.

No, Reuben!
We've been through this often enough.
Most people don't really like the taste,
and confirmed scrumpy drinkers are so rough.
Apart from a few souvenir bottles, it's
completely out of the question. It's … at variance
with the family atmosphere I'm trying to develop

– Well, the kiddies love the Giant Red Boot with play
area. They bring in the parents. I'm hoping to attract the
coach trade. Chap in the next village, swears he's made
an absolute fortune.

I'm sorry you feel like that, Reuben,
But I'm well within my rights to refuse service.
Tell me – what did they do with you the day
I came down to view this place?

Be reasonable, there's no suggestion of violence,
at least not from me – and no, I don't particularly
want to see my picture in the papers for being
cruel to a 'poor wold pensioner', but I'm confident

it won't affect my business in the long run. It may
even be good for it if the punters can see I've begun
to clean up the pub a bit.

Where? Oh God, no, not in the play area.
He'll be offering to clip the kids round their ears,
and propositioning the wives. Why me? –
He's making our lives a misery.

All right then, Reuben – It's agreed,
– keep your corner seat.
I'll order the scrumpy –

And in return –
You leave my customers alone.
– Tone down the language, Reuben, please.

Arringe Juice an Moosli

Caw, you'm lookin fair shrammed my Son
– Git down off thick tracter.

Jump up an down an flap yer arms about
fer a bit. That's right – You'm all soft you
chaps frum town. You ant got the first idea
of ow to keep yerselves warm.

Now –
What might you ave ad fer breakfast s'marnin?
Arringe Juice an Moosli!
Now there's a meal fer a workin man,
Arringe Juice an Moosli.

 – Course I seed 'Moosli' afore.
Looks like the sweepins off the granary floor if you ask me.

Thick wife a yourn'll kill thee wi all this ealthy eatin.
Arringe Juice an Moosli!

You want a breakfast as'll keep ee warm.
Parridge, or I favour a girt pan a chitlins, an
pork sausages, nicely fried, along wi a andfull
a field mushrooms. Bread and two or three
fresh eggs. All washed down wi a girt mug a tea,
wi six or seven spoonfulls a sugar in ee.

A good wold coat wudden go amiss,
an zomat to cover thee silly ead – though
there's nothin useful inside.

A layer o' goose grease smeared on the chest
is certain to keep out cold – A layer o'
goose grease an a warm woolly vest.

Smell! Don't you worry about smell my son.
She'll put up wi a bit a smell if she do love ee.

I don't old wi all this washin meeself – Taint ealthy.
Saps a man's strength. Only dirty people need cleanin.

Just you think yerself lucky you din't
work the land when I were a lad.
Hedgin and ditchin can wreak havoc wi a man.

Still, it was done religious in them days
be craftsmen who knew what they were at.
Not be some girt fool of a machine slashin away regardless.

Fair breaks my eart it do, seein the mess they do make of it.

– Just what I was tellin im this very minute, Maister.

"You git back up on thick tracter," I zaid. "You aint paid to stand
about ere lookin useless." You cain't trust these college chaps out
of your sight. Scive off soon as look at ee, they will – not like us wold
uns.

Still, you cain't really blame im – You'll never guess
what is missus give im fer brekfast s'marnin.
Arringe Juice an Moosli – I ask thee.

Arringe Juice an Moosli!

Shrammed – extremely cold
Chitlins – small intestines of a pig

23

Ethelred the Unready

Ow should I know where ee's to?
He dudden know where ee's to three-quarters of the time.

Mind we cain't complain – for tis what makes him such a tidy bowler.

See – most bowlers are creatures of habit – You line up em up
gainst any seasoned batsmen – an by and by the batsmen'll
get the measure of em.

Not im! That's the beauty of his bowling. A batsmen won't know
what he's liable to throw at em – because he dunt know.
He never thinks ahead, and he can turn on a sixpence – So
just when it looks most certain how he'll let the ball fly,
why bless you – that's the time he'll change pace and bowl underarm,
or step sideways to tread on some imaginary clod he feels is spoiling
the pitch. – It drives em mad.

The year Sydling swept all before them, we
put him into bowl against their finest – Oah, it was marvlous to see
the way he wrong-footed and unravelled them one after another,
leaving our regular chaps to step in and finish them off.

When he's on form, none can stand against him.
 – All we ave to do is get him on the bus.

Course ee's not ready.
You cain't call a man *Ethelred* and go around expectin him to be ready.
Nothing for it, I'll ave to drag im out is house.

Ethelred! Where you to?

 – Well, if you don't like the name – you
mid try bein' early a time or two – and pretty soon
you'll vind tis some other chap bein called Ethelred.

What you doin' now? Combin your hair! When chaps start taking as
long as maids to get ready it's time to
bring back National Service –
National Service an carbolic soap

No-one ever wasted time before the mirror when we washed wi carbolic.
I reckon you could ave even used
it fer sheep dip if you'd a mind – and your hair stayed where you put it
when you washed in carbolic.

Come on, Ethelred, my zon – we got a cricket match to win!

Mid – Might

25

Melchior

Melchior,
Wearing itchy new socks
bought specially for the occasion,
was shut, with others inside the
paint cupboard and ordered to be still.

It grew hot.
The audience were late and,
once settled, paid too much attention
to the infants' 'sweet' mistakes.
The wise men waited
impatient for their cue

"And from the East…."
A baby squalled,
all but drowned the words.

A teacher performed the trick
of staring at the mother
to silence the babe.

Then, in a tone much used to
the assemblies of children, repeated
"AND FROM THE EAST…."
A fight broke out,
over who should go first.
Much scuffling was heard.

Three wise fathers rushed forward,
stopped the paint cupboard from tipping
and saved the weary travellers inside.

The first emerged triumphant,
covered in pagan green.
Played to the crowd, and, in
his loud progress to the crib,
celebrated both Green Man
and Melchior.

Part 3

The Cows Who Played Bingo

I was bringing the herd in for milking. We'd just reached the most difficult part, just before the dairy, where the cows have to be driven along the main road. It's a nasty stretch, and drivers will take it at such a lick. The animals are always nervous even though there's a widish verge. This particular morning, we were moving along steadily enough when this woman comes roaring round the corner, screeched to a halt and called out she had a question needed answering. I made a show of ignoring her but she'd taken root, so I walked over to see what was so urgent.

"Do tell me, I've often wondered. – The numbers round the cows' necks. What are they for?"

I just stared at her. Here was a woman quite prepared to put a herd at risk along a main road just to get an answer to some silly question!

She obviously thought I was slow and asked her question again, only louder.

I've never used language to a woman, but I may tell you I was tempted to that day. Looking round, I saw my dogs had the herd under control, so I decided to have some fun with her.

"Cows are wonderful clever creatures, you see," I confided. "They're easily bored. It can affect the milk on occasion, so we hit on the idea of putting numbers round their necks – so they can play bingo. It's made the world of difference to them you know."

She looked at me for a fair while. Then she said, "You can't possibly believe that."

"Why not? It's the truth – ang on," I said. "I'll give you a demonstration."

Now cows are never still or silent for long, so I called out, "Two fat ladies, eighty-eight!"

One of the cows mooed.

"There you are! She knows her number, didn't I tell you? Well done, girl."

"I'm sure your cows are very intelligent… but," and she paused, "they do not have the capacity to memorise or read numbers, so they simply cannot play bingo."

She told me this as though breaking some awful news to a child.

"Well, I'm blessed how they do it then. Go on, get out of your car and see for yourself that she's got eighty-eight round er neck."

I knew of course that this woman was as likely to pick her way through mud and manure as I am to ever walk on solid gold.

"I tell you what, let's try again," I said. "What number shall we choose eh?"

And I call out, "Legs Eleven." This time, one cow makes a noise, and another shakes her head, so I make out there's an argument going on.

"You need to keep your wits about you, for not only are cows wonderful intelligent – they're shocking cheats!"

"It's just coincidence the cows make those noises when you call out numbers – you do know that don't you? "

And at that the poor woman drove off, believing that in the heart of the Dorset Countryside was a man who believed his cows could play Bingo.

Photo of Lil Puckett, source of the Dairyman's Story,
retold as The Cows Who Played Bingo.

The Colorado Beetle Craze

Mickey: I bin looking for a Colorado Beetle all summer. We all ave. Ever since Derek Chant's cousin saw a poster warnin they were pests that could destroy potato crops, an offerin a reward of £5 for every one handed into a Police Station. Five pounds for some ordinary old black beetle with yellow stripes on. We were going to keep it secret, Stuart, Derek Chant an me, but Derek Chant's sister told the girls, an there was a race on to see who could find a Colorado Beetle first. Girls are rubbish spies. My Granfer says he'd rather have the bindweed in his garden any day. They made a right mess not knowing how to look proper, so we all got banned. It dint stop me though, I'm careful I don't get caught.

    Then today, just as I was givin up hope, I saw a beetle scuttlin under the lettuces, a black beetle, exactly the same as Derek Chant's cousin saw on the poster, and with a streak of yellow on it. I got excited, thinking I'd found a Colorado Beetle and would get my five pounds after all but it turned out the yellow was a bit of old leaf an I lost my temper. "I bet they got hundreds in Colorado!" I shouted. "You'd think they'd let just one of them come over here so I could get my five pounds." All summer I been lookin – an that beetle looked exactly like the one on the poster, except for the stripes. I bet nobody could tell difference. An that's when I remembered Stuart'ud had to buy a whole tin of yellow enamel paint for a tiny strip on one of his models, an I thought I'm much better than him, I bet I could paint two thin straight lines of yellow paint down this beetle an no-one would notice it want real.

    They don't alf wriggle beetles. One of the lines went wrong, and I had to wipe the paint off an spit on the beetle to clean it. I didn't hurt it, I don't like people that go round hurtin things just for fun. It din't much like being held, but I had to wait until it was dry before I put it in the old biscuit tin with holes in.

Now I can take it up to Mr Alford to claim my five pounds. The door's always locked so I hope he's in. Spends his life drinking cups of tea, my dad says.

[Mickey hammers on door.]

Mickey: Mr Alford! Mr Alford. I found a Colorado Beetle and I've come for my five pounds. Mr Alford. You in there, Mr Alford?"

[Mickey moves to peer over the top of a highish window. Mr Alford puts his cup of tea down, unbolts and clanks open the door.]

Mickey: I come for my five pounds, Mr Alford. I got the beetle in this tin, with some potato leaves. That's what they eat you know, he'll probably chomp through that lot in next to no time, so I'll bring up some more tomorrow but whatever you do, don't let im out. If just one gets out, they'll spread like wildfire, an there'll be no tiddies for makin chips this year – you like your chips don't you Mr Alford? You don't want to let him escape then, you'd never live it down, just take a quick look to make sure I'm tellin you the truth an it really is a Colorado Beetle, because I tell you Mr Alford he's a real pest that beetle.

Policeman: Not the only pest round here, is he, Mickey? I've got a village full of them, wrecking people's gardens and driving farmers mad. You kids have done more damage than any number of Colorado Beetles. So, whose garden you found this one in then?

Mickey: Ours, Mr Alford, honest. It was scuttling under a lettuce, on his way through to the potatoes I reckon, cause that's what they eat. It says so on the poster.

Policeman: It's a male then, Mickey? I didn't realise you were such an expert on the subject.

32

Mickey:	I was one of the very first people Derek Chant told, Mr Alford, so I got the information straight. It might be a female. It's very hard to tell with beetles. Would I get more for a female? I ought to really, cause a female could get out there and lay hundreds and hundreds of eggs and do a lot more damage, but I'll leave that up to you to decide cause I know you wouldn't try and cheat anyone. Careful how you open that tin now.
Policeman:	I need to have a good look, Mickey, I'm not going to hand over five pounds just like that. Even if you have found something that looks like it might be a Colorado Beetle, I'll have to send it off and get it checked.
Mickey:	They'll have spread everywhere by then, Mr Alford. I think you an me have got to act fast to stop them spreading.
Policeman:	Well, lets just make sure we've actually got a Colorado Beetle, before we get too excited about it.

[He moves the leaves around, spots the beetle, and picks it up to have a closer look.]

Policeman:	*[After several minutes]* No, I'm sorry, Mickey. I don't think this is a Colorado Beetle we got here.
Mickey:	Yes, yes it is. A black shiny beetle with yellow stripes that lives on potato leaves, just like it says on the poster.
Policeman:	No. You see, Mickey, I think what we got here is a stink beetle. You want to know why I'm so sure it's a stink beetle – because I can still smell the paint! – I tell you what though, Mickey. I'll give you half a crown for it, so I can take it into the station in Dorchester and try it on them. Every child in Dorset's been searchin for Colorado Beetles this summer holiday – and you're the only lad with enough gump to make your own.

33

The Good Shepherd

First Woman: Good Lord he's decided what? Keep animals on sacred ground. It's the daftest idea I ever heard – Besides being sacrilegious, who wants to risk stepping in a sheep's turd?

I bet a pound to a penny Tizard's behind it, he'll do anything to squirm out of a bit of honest toil – and this latest trick. Fair makes my blood boil.

Has the vicar any notion of how sheep smell? His is the final decision after all – Don't you worry I'm going up directly to tell him straight to his face – And he better have a damn good excuse. That's all I can say.

And you got all this Tomfoolery from the vicar himself? All that education – and he's not safe left to tie his own shoelaces.

Second Woman: "The churchyard is dreadfully overgrown."

First Woman: Oh, he's noticed then.

Second Woman: "It's too much for one man to manage."

First Woman: It's too much for Tizard, that's true.

Second Woman: He thinks it will make a "charming pastoral scene."

First Woman: Dear God, what can the man mean? – Two years he's lived here, and what he knows of the country could be writ on a stamp and still leave room for the Queen.

Second Woman: He also said, "We often refer to Our Lord as 'the Good Shepherd.'" So it seems to him highly appropriate that we should have sheep grazing contentedly round our church. He went on for a bit. I didn't really listen after that – But I thought you ought to know.

First Woman: He does go on – I wonder if he's like it at home. If so, it's no surprise to me they've never had any children. By the time he's finished his "For what we are about to receives," she must be raking through the ashes.

34

Of course, we'll have to change his mind.
There's enough Heathens round here without him
encouraging them. What we do is make a great fuss –
he's a coward at heart and he won't want to cross us.

The Drowners in the Water Meadow

I was a solitary child, given to
wandering off on my own and
I was fascinated by water, as a lot of
children are; they find themselves drawn to it.

I was drawn especially to the shallow covering
of water meadows in flood. I loved to go there when
the storm was spent. The surface of the water turns
almost silver in the sun, and looking
down you will see grass swaying
under water like seaweed.
I was careful not to
go near the river or
the ditches, but the
danger I was warned of
was not water.

There are beautiful people who live in
the water, it was said. Most of the time they are
confined to the river, but when this floods, they
can move out into the water meadows. These
are beautiful people, with beautiful children
of their own, but the Drowners are entranced
by village children, and if they get the chance

THE DROWNERS & MERCY 2002

will lure them deeper and deeper into the water.

The Drowners will leave a bright necklace or a toy in the shallows, and then, when a child stoops for it, they find it is out of reach. They walk a little deeper into the water, and find time and time again that the treasure lies tantalisingly close but just beyond them.

This is how the Drowners entice. A child may find their foot is caught around a root, or feel themselves sinking further and further into the mud, for that is another danger of these shallow floods. They may see a beautiful lady, but if she touches them they will find her deadly cold.

If these children are lucky, someone going along the road will see, and run to pull them from the water. If not, they will drown, or be carried off to heavens only know where. They will be quite lost to their family and friends."

Hiring Fair: Isaac Hallet, shepherd, and his collie

Oh – she's a dog to treasure this one – worth six men when she's workin flat out – She'd give er life blood to protect the flock – an fly! There's not a dog can touch her. They get two fer the price a one when they hire us – don't they, Jess.

Now, tis a funny thing ... but I always felt t'was she that chose me rather than t'other way round.

True, I was on the look out fer another dog to train up, an I was over at Shep'erd Aitkins avin a look at the latest litter off old Sally. Not that I eld out any hopes of bein able to afford one mind. Shep'erds ud come from all over to get one a they dogs off im – but I always like to take a look. Marvellous litter, marvellous. I said to im – you've got a champion or two there.

An then this tiny scrap of a thing starts pullin at my bootlaces – "Don't let er bother you. Kick it away," ee says. "Tis the runt a the litter an I'm ashamed to ave it in the yard. I'll get rid of it directly."

But there was somethin about thik particular scrap a fur I took to. She was pullin somethin tenacious on my bootlaces an pretty soon she'd worked out ow to get one of em loose. So I picked er up an said twas a shame, an peraps if someone took the trouble to feed er up she'd come on by an by.

"Well," ee said, "if you think you can make anythin of it you can ave er fer nothin – er's practically weaned, but don't you durst tell anyone you ad er off I for it ud ruin my reputation."

I took some leg pullin on account a she I may tell you – carryin er round an feedin er any little bits an bobs I could scrounge. Everyone said I was soft and a shepherd cain't afford to be so sentimental. But they weren't laughing the next spring when they seed er workin alongside my other dogs – pickin up everything they ad to show er quick as you please.

Shep'erd Aitkin come over when he seed us at Dorchester market an ee says to me, ee says, "I must ave bin a fool to let you ave thik dog fer nuthin. I ope you ant never told anyone I give such a dog away," which course I adden – an I wudden be telling you now if I wasn't sure you could hold a story.

Now! Ere's somethin that'll make you laugh. While we was talkin, without either of us avin the first idea of what she was up too, Jess ere slipped round an catch im a nip on the back of is leg the like a which I'd never seed er give afore or since. She won't even lose patience wi

the tups normally, got the best temperament you'll ever seen in a dog – but just that one time she got Shep'erd Aitkin fair an square – ant ever forgot im see, though ee never touched er far as I knew.

They say elephants ave got famous good memories – tidden nothin compared to a collie. I've known a collie 'old a grudge for a good ten years 'fore gettin their own back on someone who'd bin unkind to em.

But be kind, an treat em decent, you'll never find loyalty like it – idden that right, Jess?"

Photo of Brian Caddy and Jess. Brian is a local poet and performer, author of 'River King' and other works.

Sources of Stories

The following pages are for everyone who has asked to know more about where my stories come from. The stories, and the ingredients for my stories, are, in the main, drawn from the Stratton of my memory, from Dorset more generally, and from working in local hospitals, particularly Damers. I've used common West Country names haphazardly, except in Acknowledgements.

My memory is not a tidy or a complete thing. It can wander off and forget itself, but, just as some people have an ear for music, I have an ear for a good story and the poetry of human speech.

An Abused Wife's Prayer Modelled on *The Wreckers' Prayer*. Working in hospitals, people share their happiest stories with you, and also their saddest.

Young Mother & Great Grandmother I waitressed alongside someone. She talked of the time she'd had to seek help for her children, and the business of 'managing'. I knew that word, and everything it brought in its wake. Sometime later, I heard a speaker on the radio who was dismissive of the idea of poverty in modern Britain. I thought of her. As I started thinking through the poem, I knew there would need to be a counter voice. Someone who felt every bit as strongly as the Young Mother did, but believed her to be wrong. Not someone on the radio but in the same family, perhaps even in the same house. Some of the earliest readings with Joy Caddy as Great Grandmother revealed the Young Mother part needed strengthening.

Tick Tock Story heard in Damers Hospital and retold as a poem.

Poacher All countryman like to think themselves capable of laying their hands on the odd bird or rabbit, should the need arise, and it's a well-known fact that the world is full of suicidal trout. My Poacher was garnered from overheard conversations between older men in Stratton and Damers Hospital.

Granny Collins House Classic house on the edge of a village and a childhood fear, enclosed in the pearl of a poem.

Weymouth Maid and Empty Vessels This is an improvement on life. I wrote of a woman who moves from Weymouth to the country on marriage, as my mother did, and meets with a father-in-law, who, though initially resistant, would be kind and warm to her over time, becoming her protector. Empty vessels is also about women engaged in field work.

Dorset Ophelier I became fascinated by how a practical Dorset woman would have spoken to Shakespeare's Ophelia and doubtless tried to take her in hand.

I Before E Plays with the business of the two languages, Dorset and Standard English, their uneasy co-existence, the back-and-forth policing of them, and the fun that is to be had. My own father liked tongue-twisters, poems and word play, but was not the confident father of the poem.

Morning Maister That which is said behind the backs of men who may imagine themselves more respected than they are. The sentiments overheard numerous times and distilled into a single poem.

Incomer The West Country richness of language extends to insult – and, having directed some of the best insults at my Incomer, I give her the best retort.

Rueben An old man seen disconsolately blowing froth around the top of his beer, sat by himself in the corner of a once-quiet pub, as the fad to attract families took off. I occasionally thought of him, and of all the new Landlords in pubs determined to make a success of things. What if, instead of a quietly gloomy regular, a Landlord found he'd inherited a rebellious relic of one of the real old spit-and-sawdust sanctuaries? I found the voice of my Landlord in Andy Venton, who remains the best performer of Rueben and, once I had the Landlord's voice, I could envisage the back-and-forth of their battle.

Arringe Juice an Moosli is a gift of a poem that practically wrote itself. I started on a piece, comparing the breakfasts people once ate when doing physically demanding work outside in the bitter cold to the breakfasts of today. I thought of the men who drove tractors when there was no protective cab, and remembered a litany of advice overheard, the retelling of earlier hardships, and the mourning for a world where things were done properly. An experienced agricultural worker, then, and who is he tutoring? A younger man, new to the land, and there will be kindness wrapped in remorseless rough teasing, before they are called to order for wasting time. Odd memories surfaced – the smell of goose grease which I had sold while working in a chemist and never forgot, and I knew exactly how the older man would view any delicacy about smell.

Brian Caddy performed 'Arringe Juice an Moosli' while it was being polished, and has performed it in and around Dorset ever since, adding his marvellous introduction.

Ethelred the Unready I can't name any of the cricketers who inspired Ethelred. He is an amalgam of bowlers seen catching out batsmen with odd or unpredictable throws. I asked myself, what if a bowler's unpredictability was a character trait rather than a tactic? Such a man could be a genius on the pitch and a nightmare off it. I'd heard the nickname Ethelred used to tease someone for always being late and it was the perfect name for my bowler. Talk of carbolic soap and the need to bring back National Service were hardy perennials during the 1960s.

I wrote the poem with Brian Caddy's voice in mind.

Melchior is the sum of all Nativity Plays ever watched. I'm a sucker for adenoidal Angels, tea-towel Shepherds and belligerent Wise Men. I was once lucky enough to see a Wise Man get poster paint tipped on him in rehearsal. In 'Melchior' it happens on the night. I also love the way different, more raucous traditions get celebrated at Christmas.

The Cows who Played Bingo My retelling of a story told by Lil Puckett, my Grandfather's second wife – 'Our Grandmother', as shared by Joy Parsons. Lil had a range of cracking stories and anecdotes, including a very funny but creepy story about grave robbers, which I have never been able to do justice to.

The Good Shepherd As a child, I was a bell ringer and member of the choir in Stratton and Bradford Peverell churches. I have clear memories both of a disagreement about whether sheep should be used to keep grass down in a churchyard, and of the sort of sturdy women who inhabit churches. For my story, I added a vicar under siege, and someone thought not to be keeping the grass under control who I gave the surname Tizard as a play on words.

The Drowners in the Water Meadows Retelling of a story told by an older woman, who was living in one of houses near the milking parlour at the time. I have no idea who she was, which is a shame, as I should like to credit her in the same way as I have Lil Puckett. I think there were damsons in her garden, but that is not much help.

Isaac Hallett Shepherd – part of 'Hiring Fair' – Brian Caddy has a delightful collie, Jess, and was happy for her to take part. So I wrote a story for Brian to tell the audience (and Chris Pullen's agricultural labourer) of how he, as Isaac, came to own such a marvellous dog. The story was drawn from numerous overheard debates and stories about how to choose a good dog, or whether its best for a dog to choose you.

The Colorado Beetle Craze was woven from memories of the endless days of a Summer's holiday, of news passed from child to child of a poster that promised £5 for a Colorado Beetle, of rummaging through gardens in search of the marvellous beetle, and our rummagings not being universally popular with gardeners. This, twinned with a mother's knowledge that, with £5 at stake, somewhere or other there would be a child mischievous and bright enough to try and pass off some other beetle as the infamous Colorado.

My Place, The Cut of Me Jib and The West Country Ages of Man are observed pieces.

Performers' place in the shaping of stories. I like being able to try new writing on an audience to see what works, what doesn't, and what could be improved. I may change a piece of writing substantially during this process, so the performers named played a part in my shaping of the poems.